Book 2

Coloring Pages For Kids Birds Coloring Book

Coloring Books for Kids

By Gala Publication

Published by:

Gala Publication

ISBN-13: 978- 1508659433
ISBN-10: 1508659435

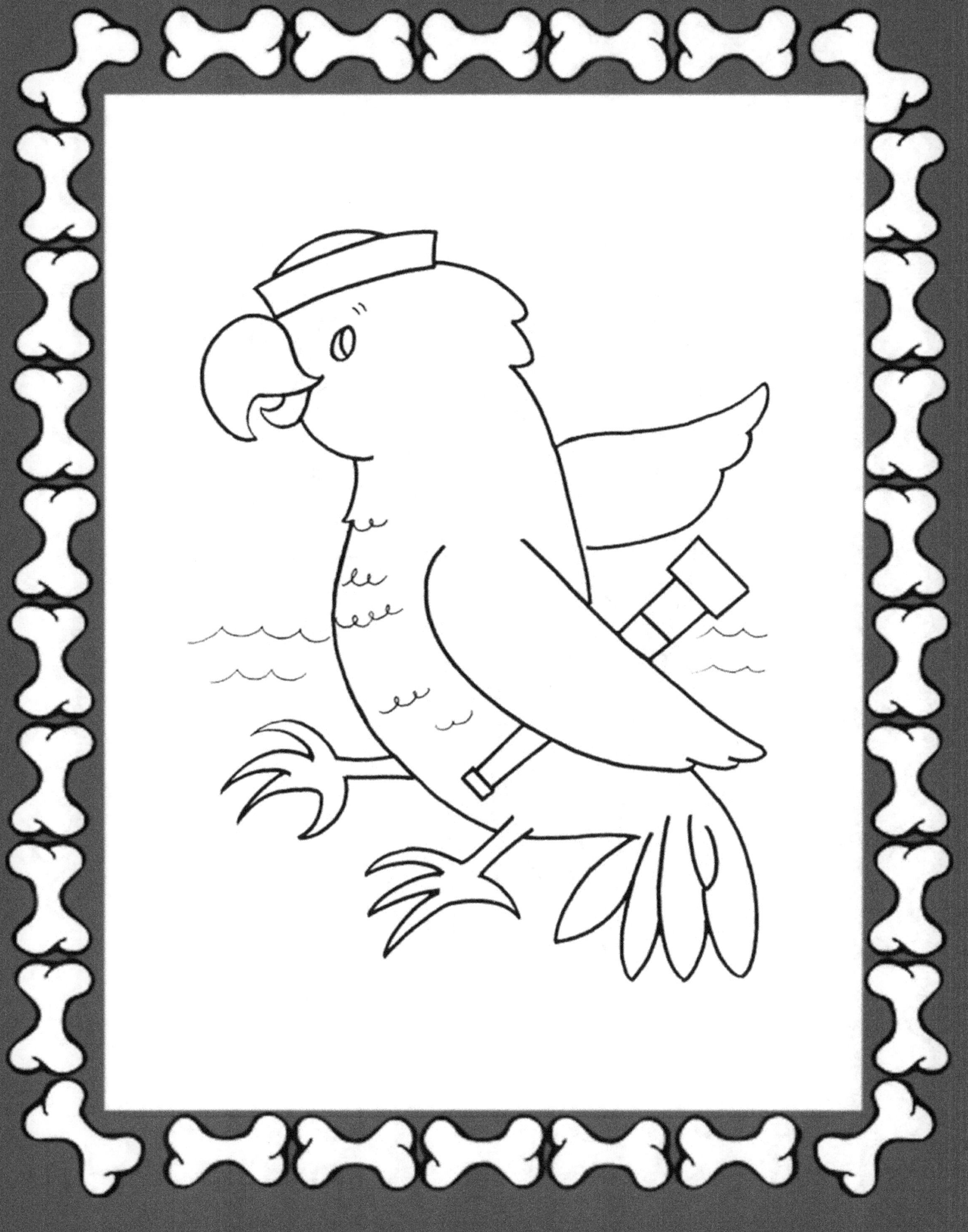

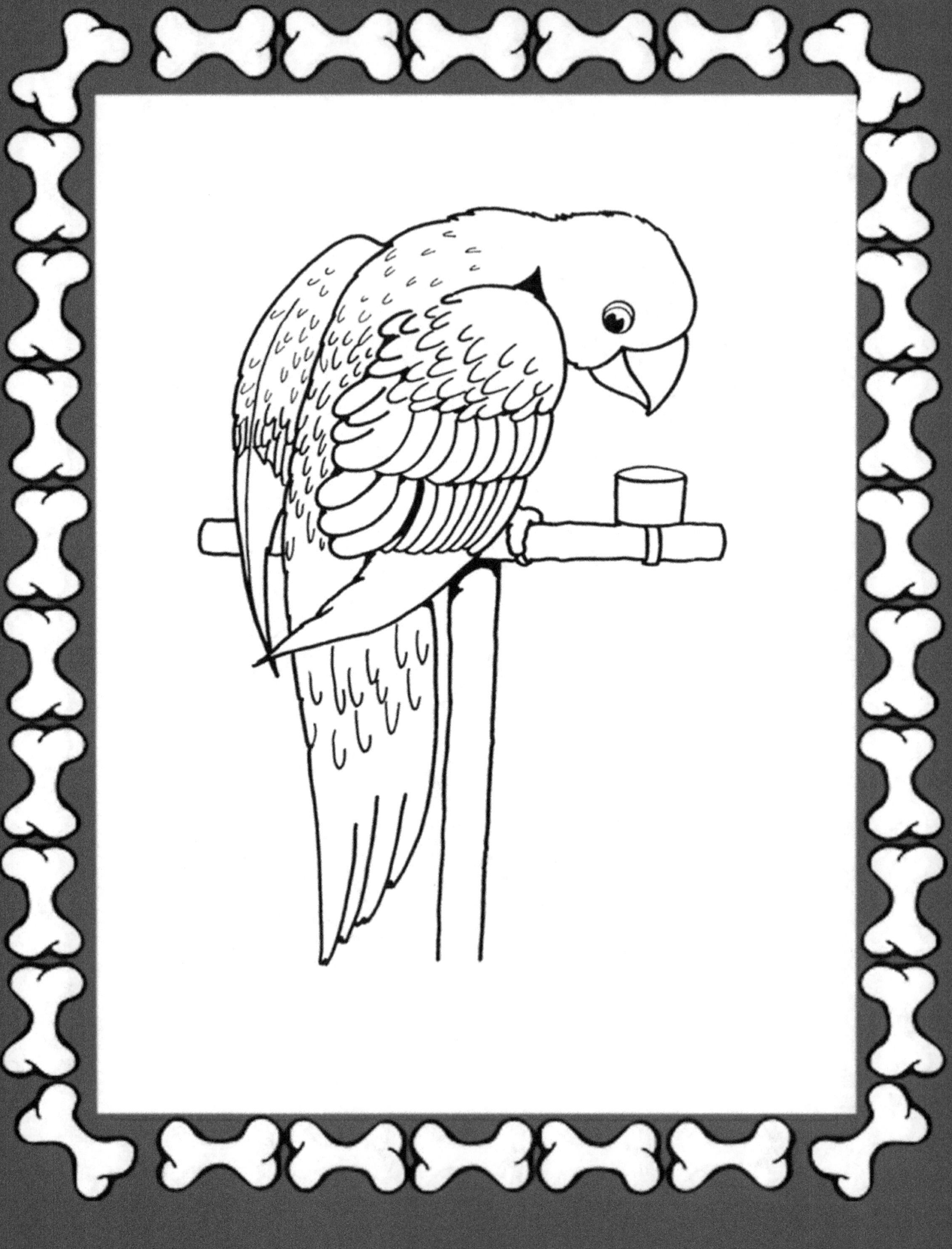

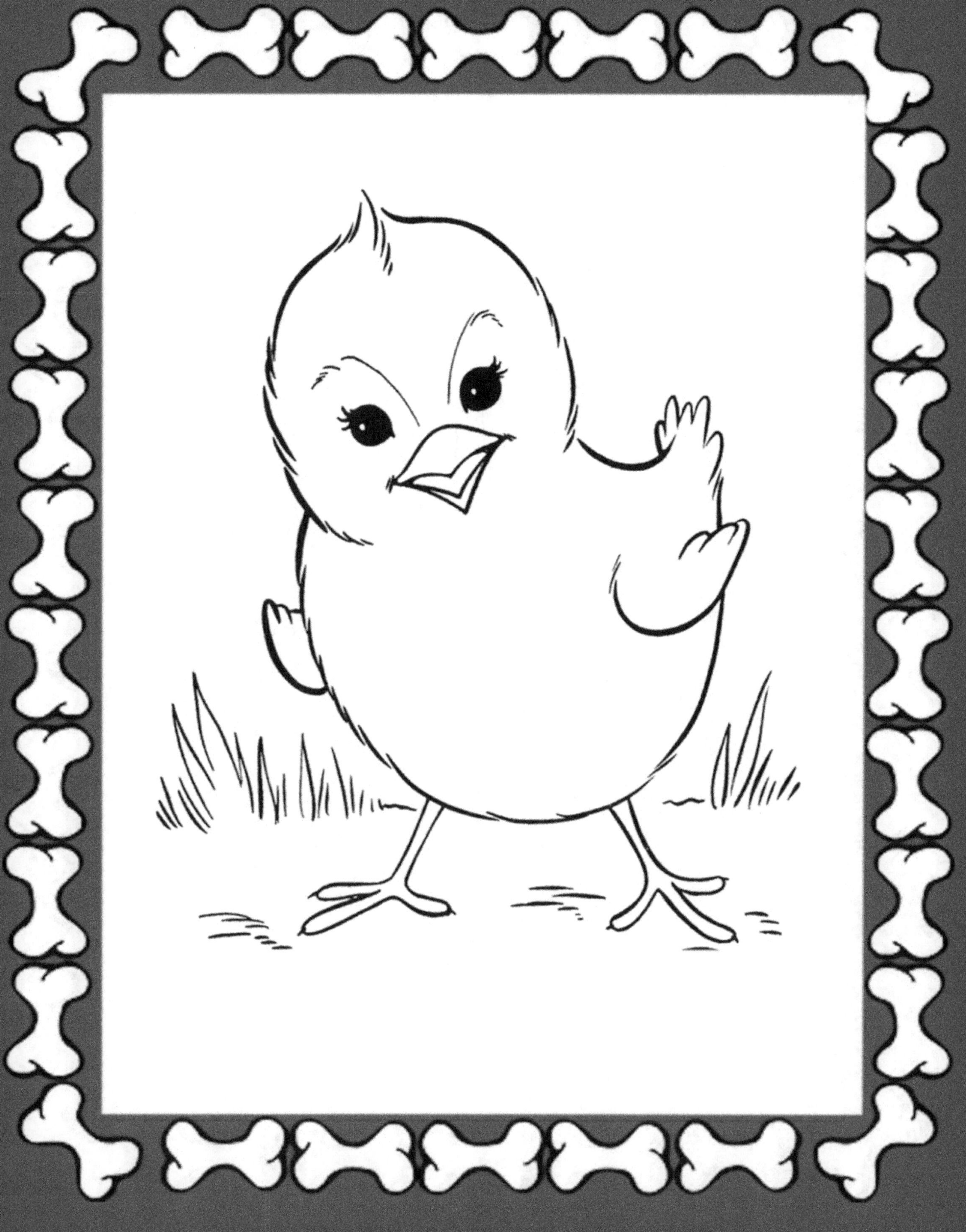

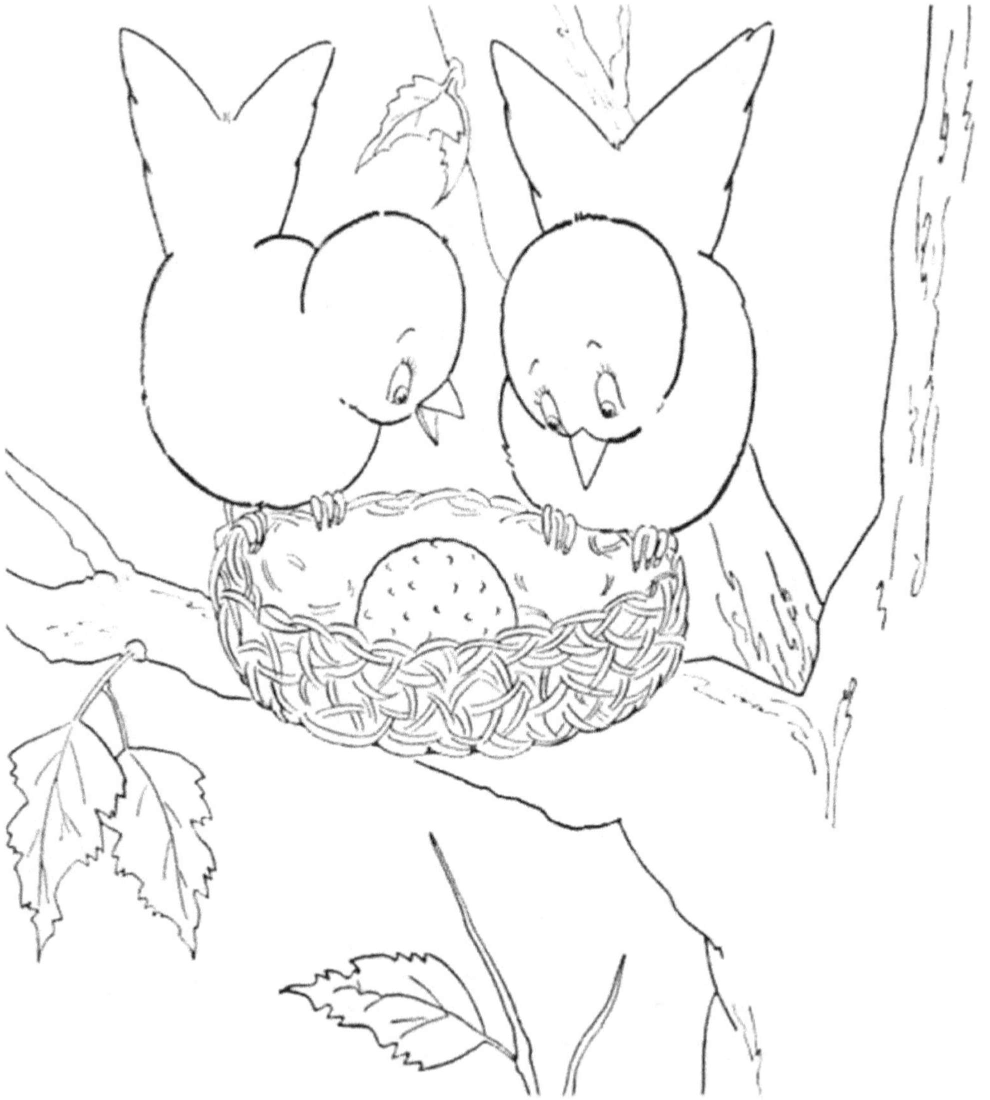

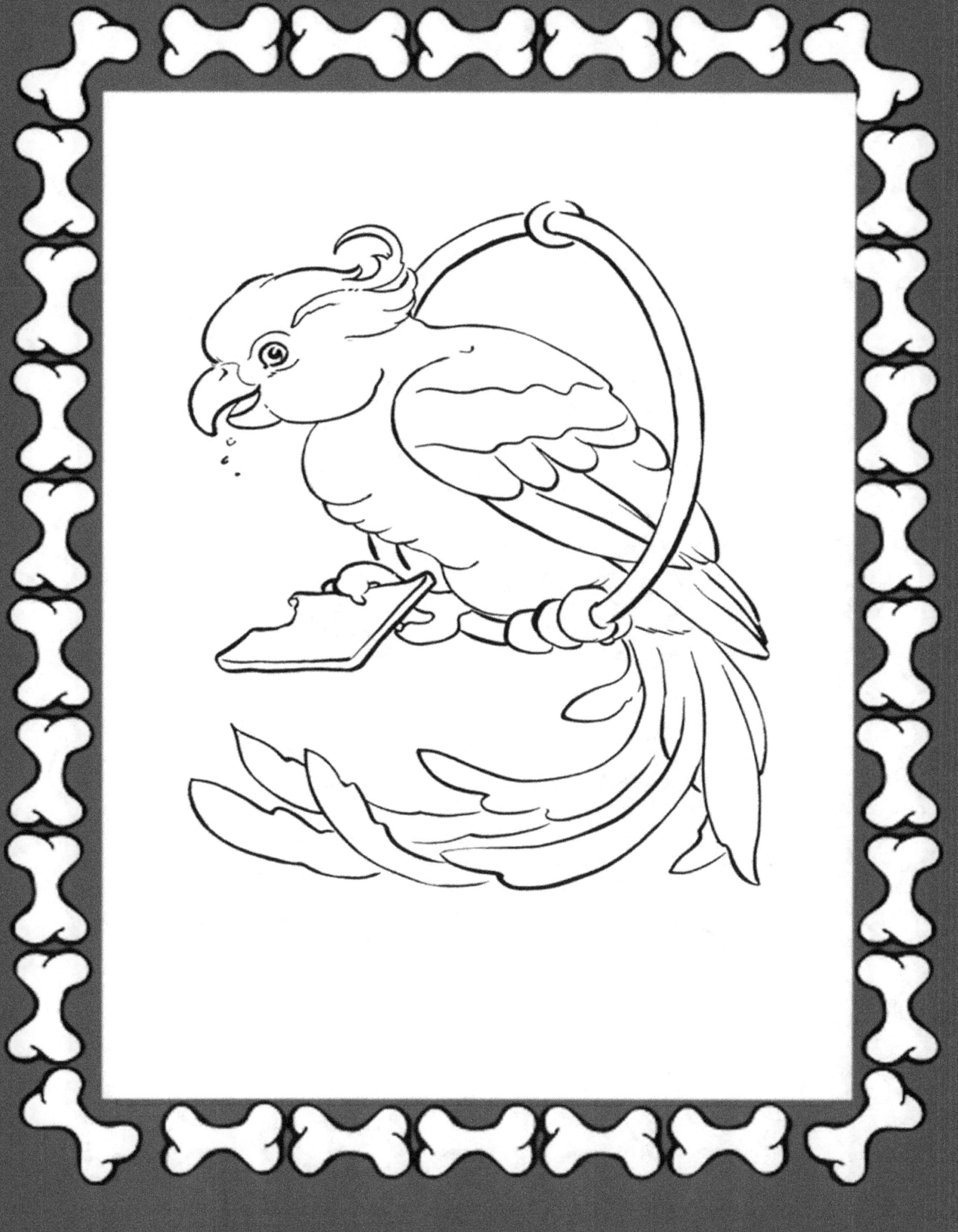

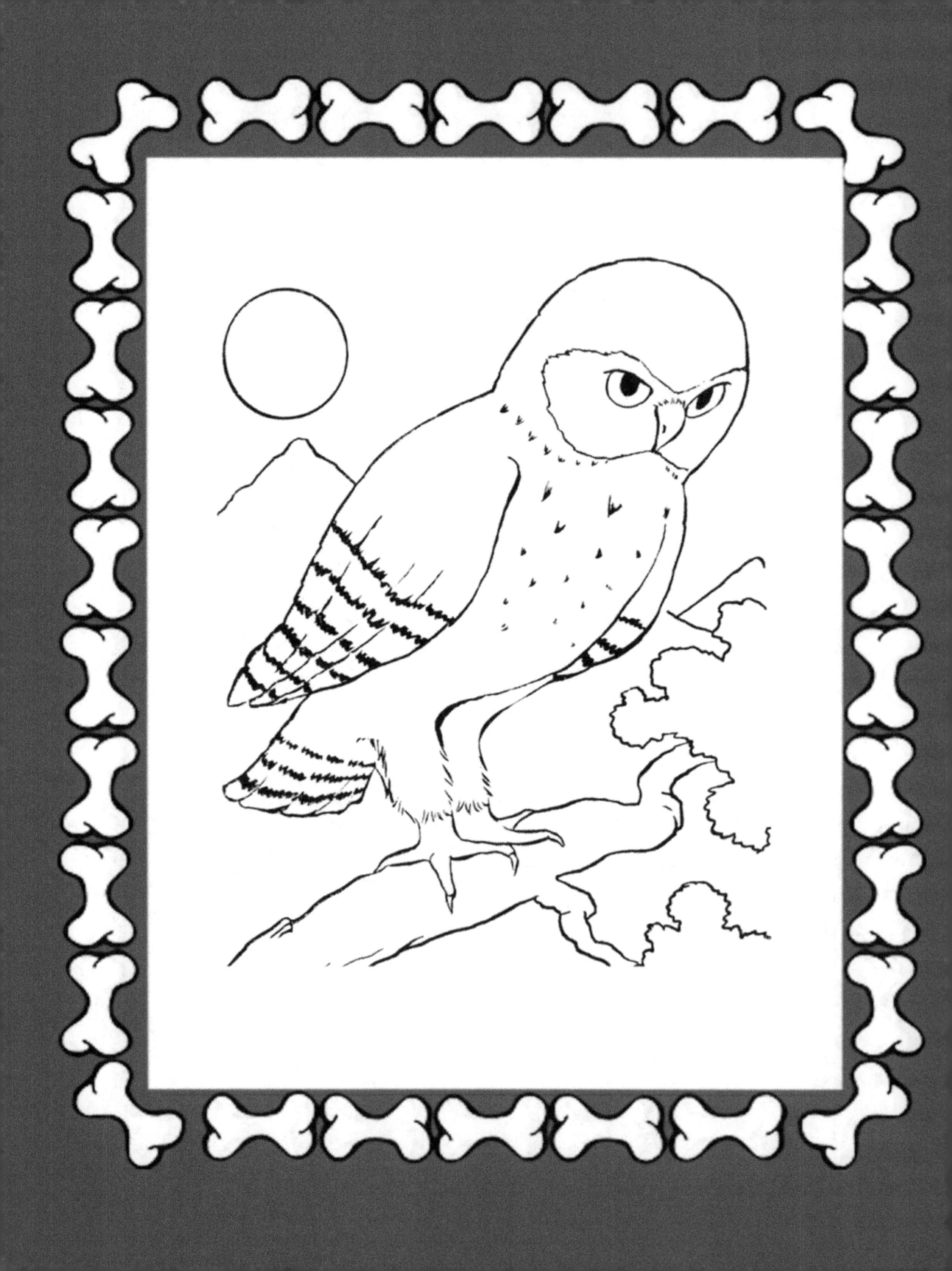

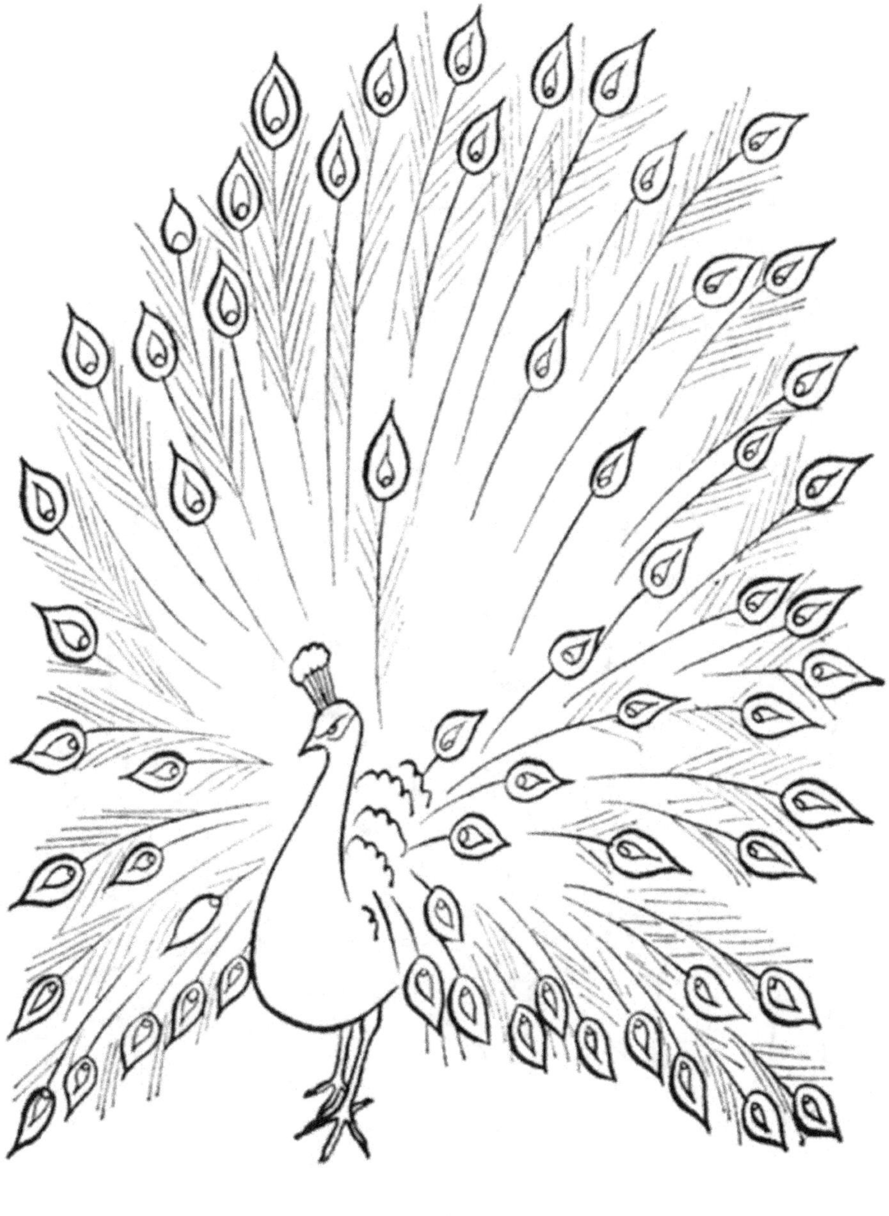

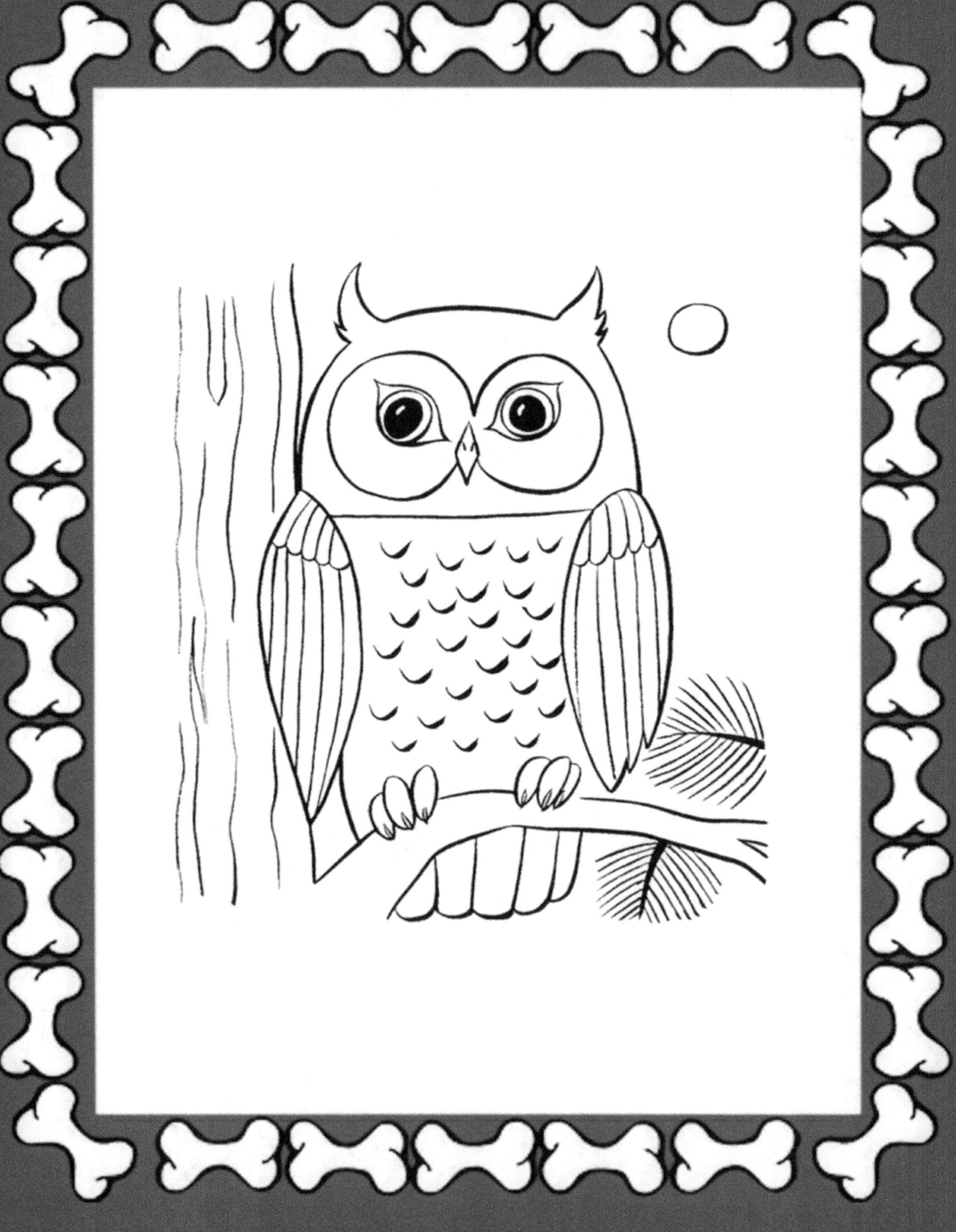

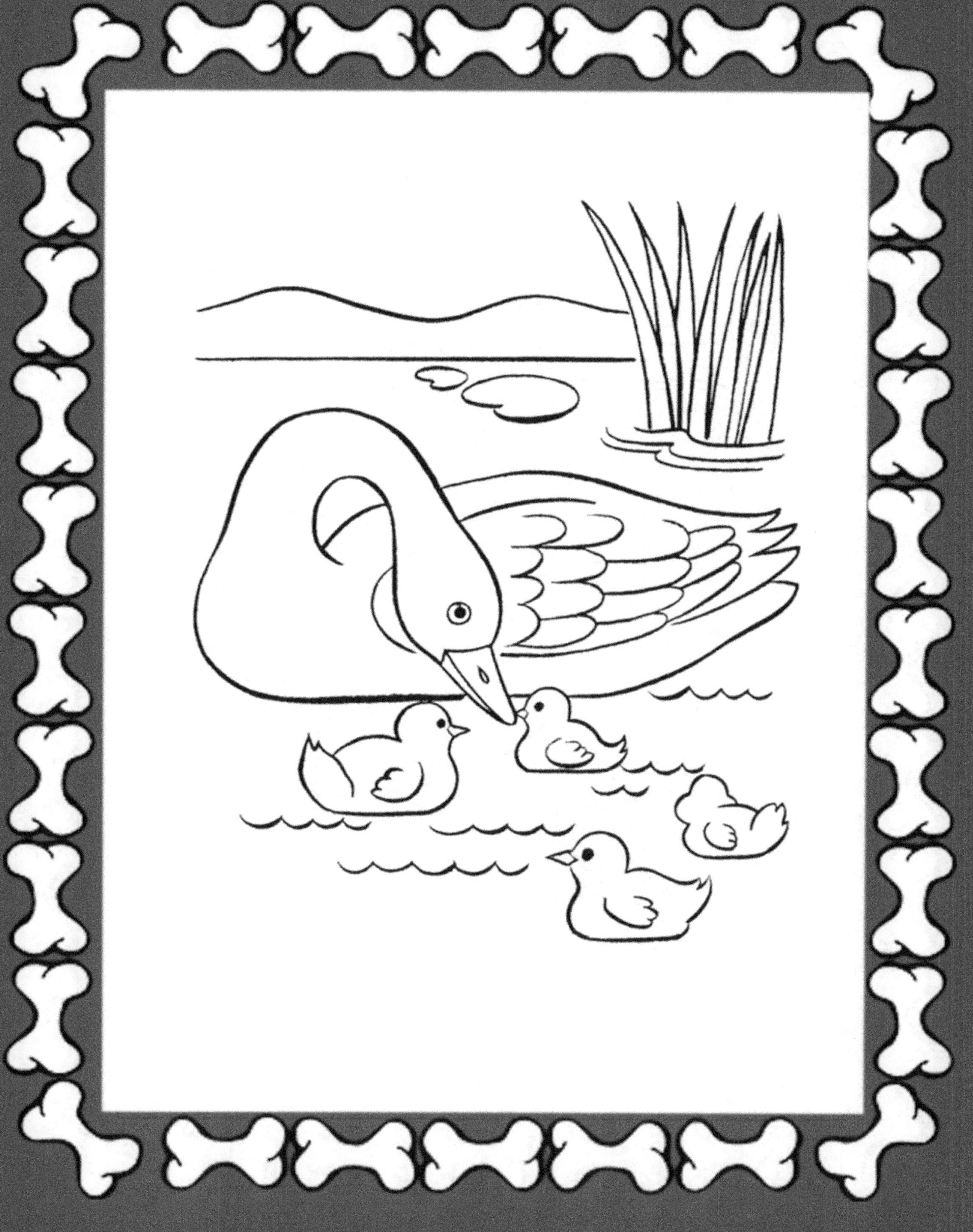

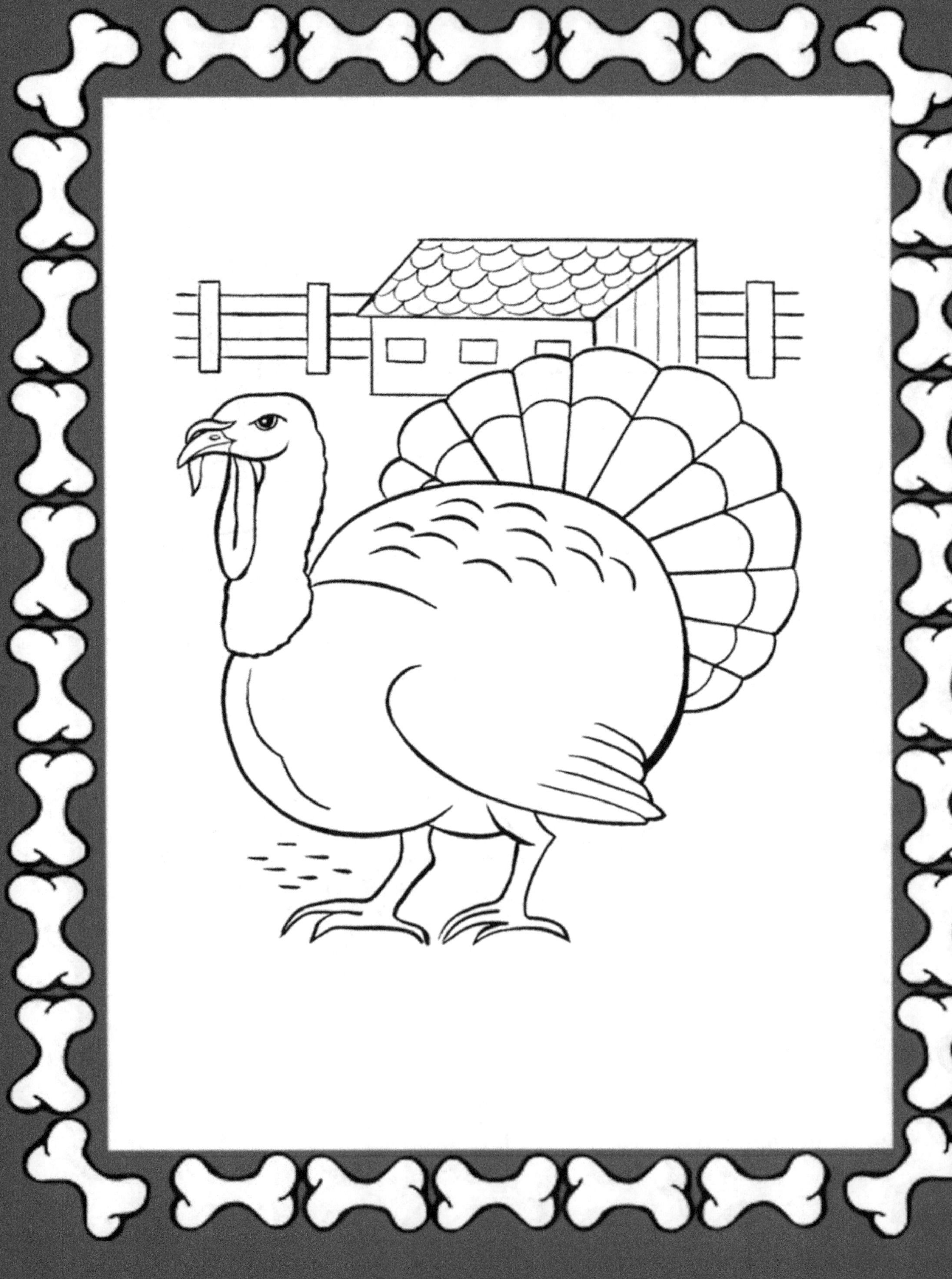

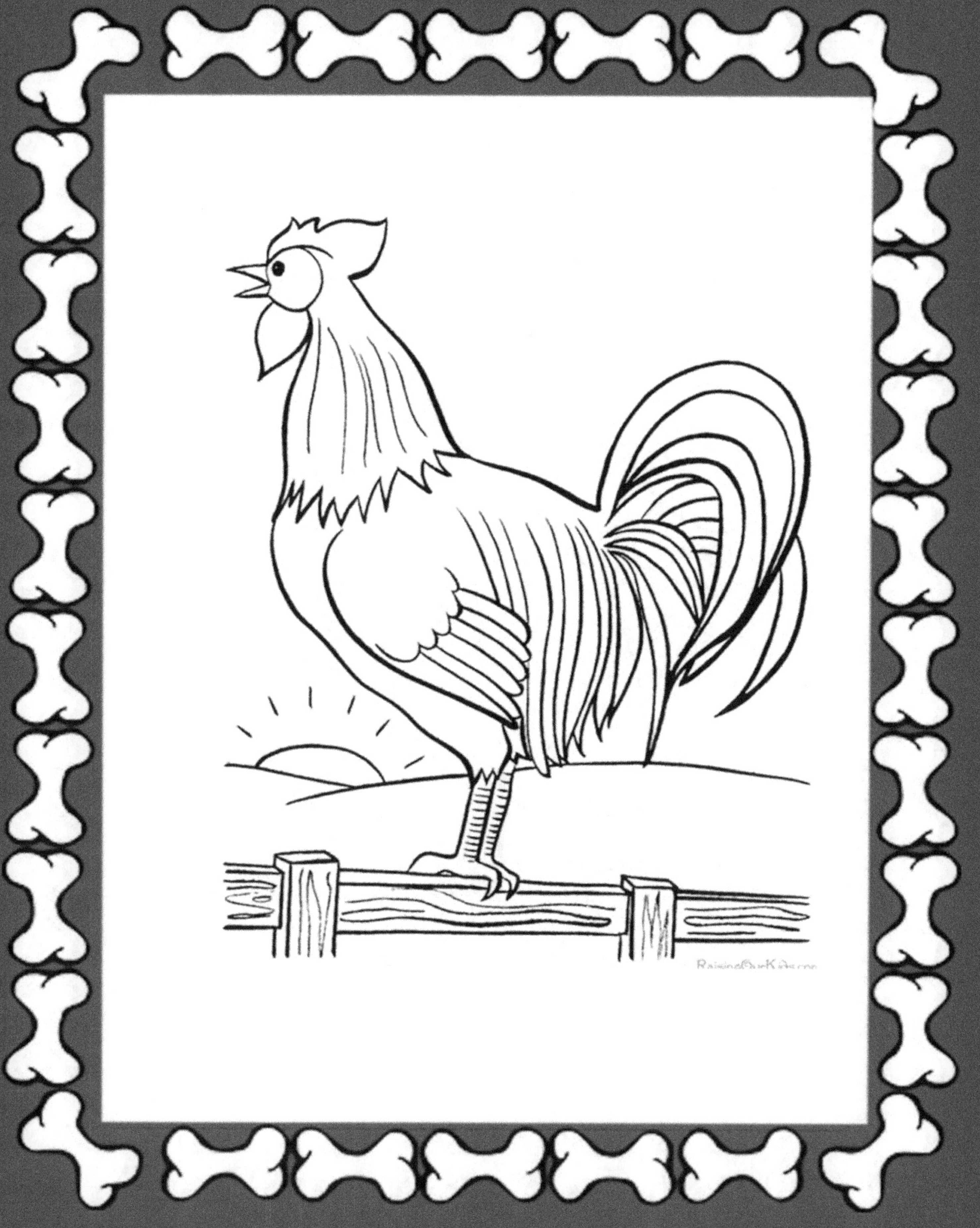

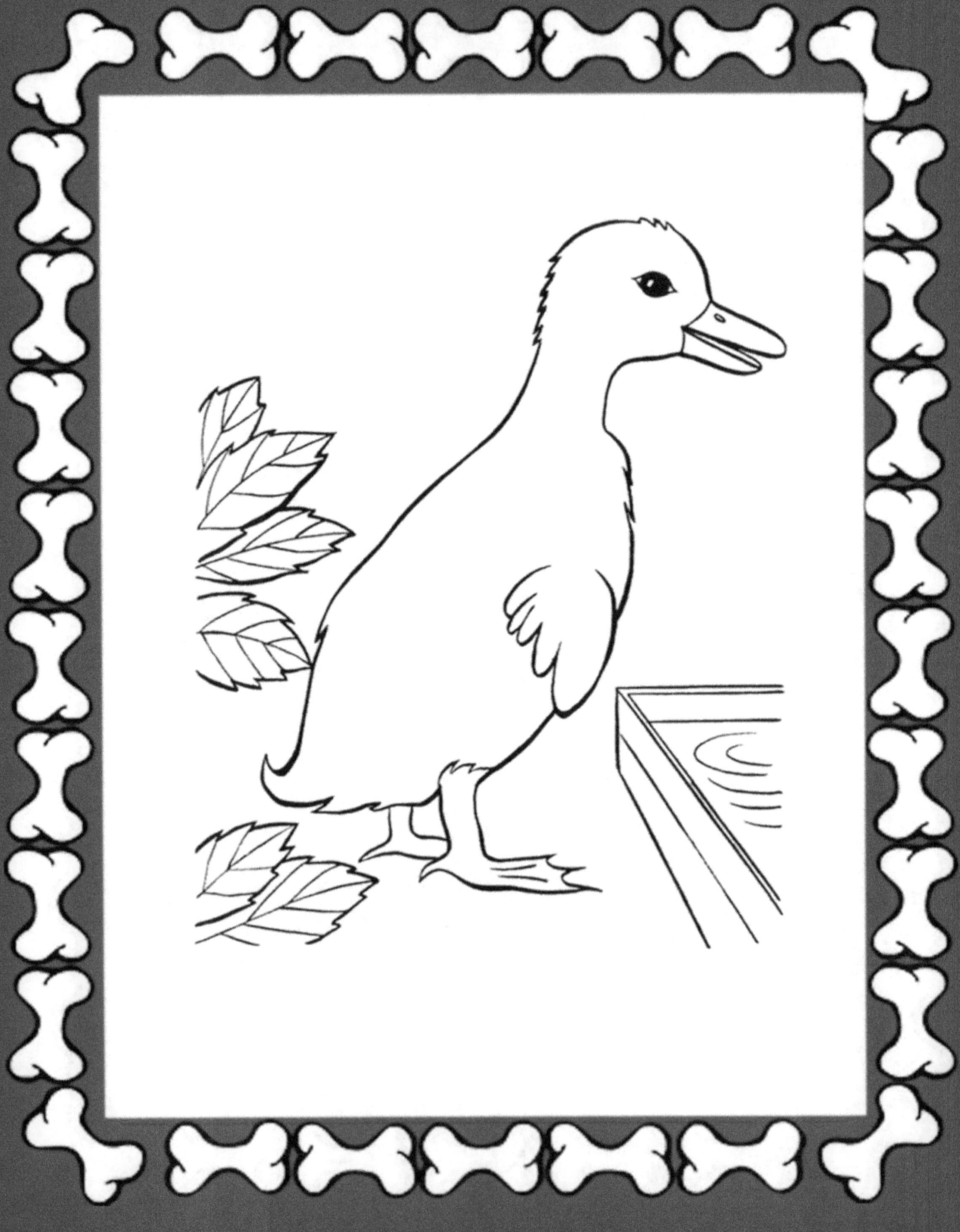

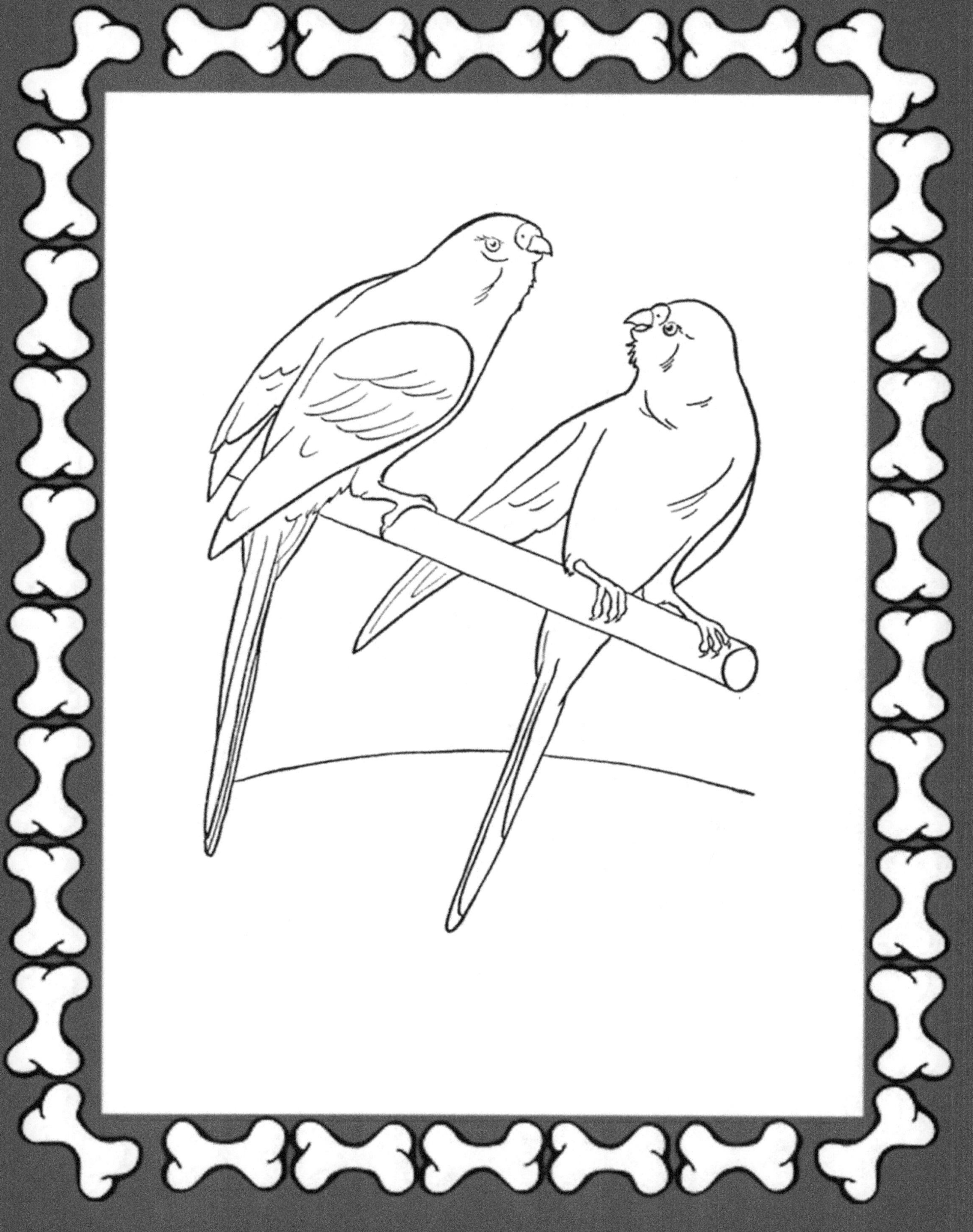

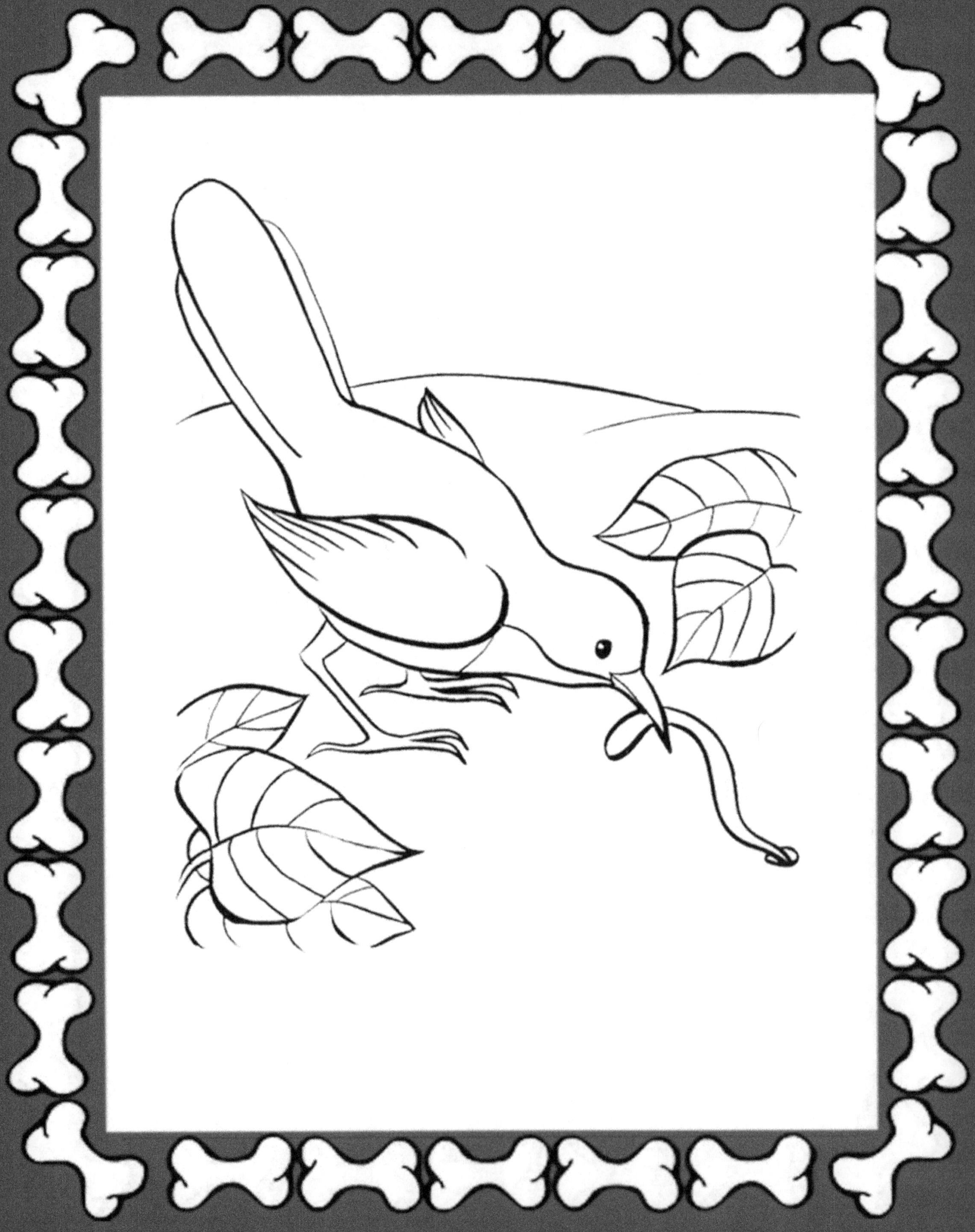

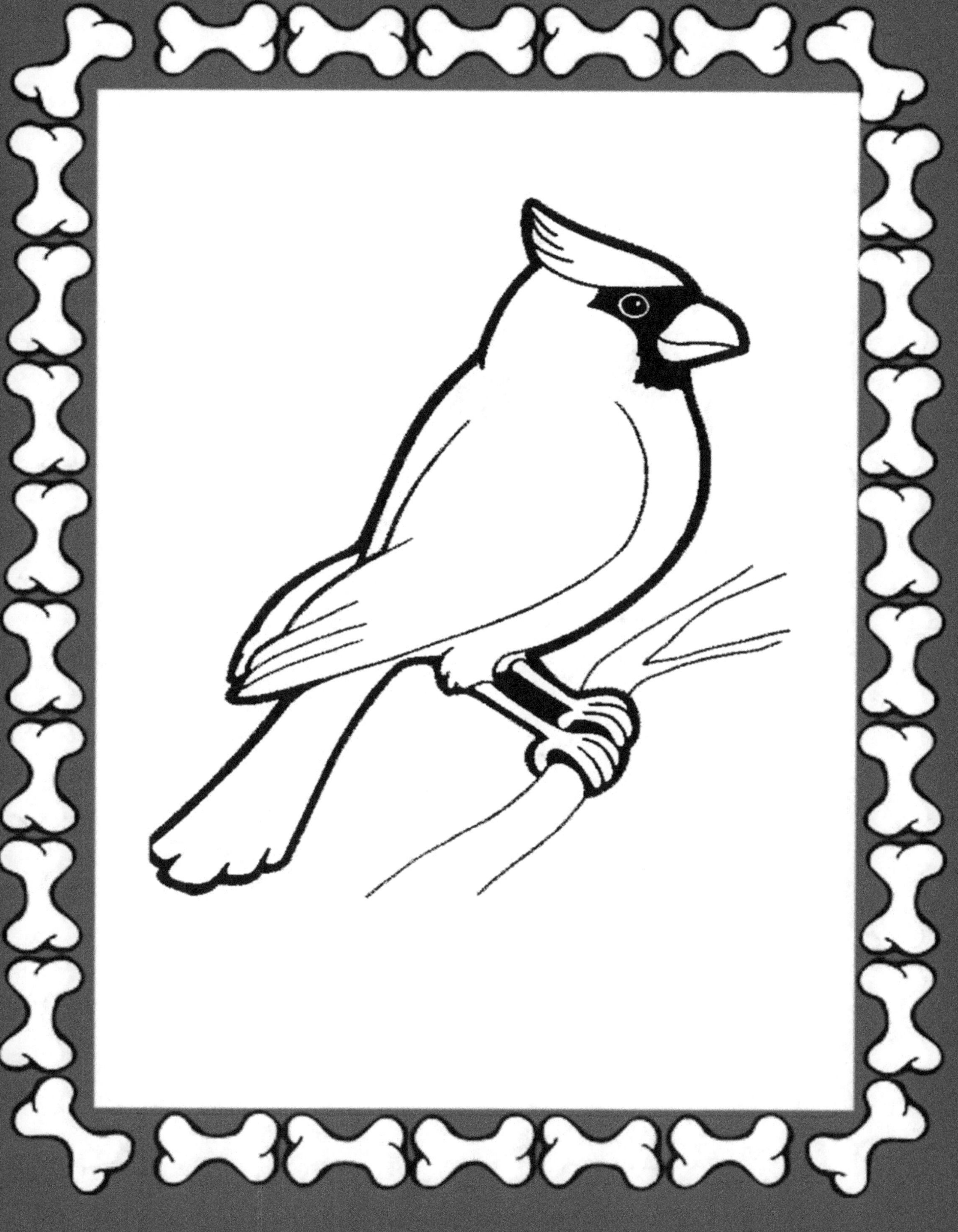

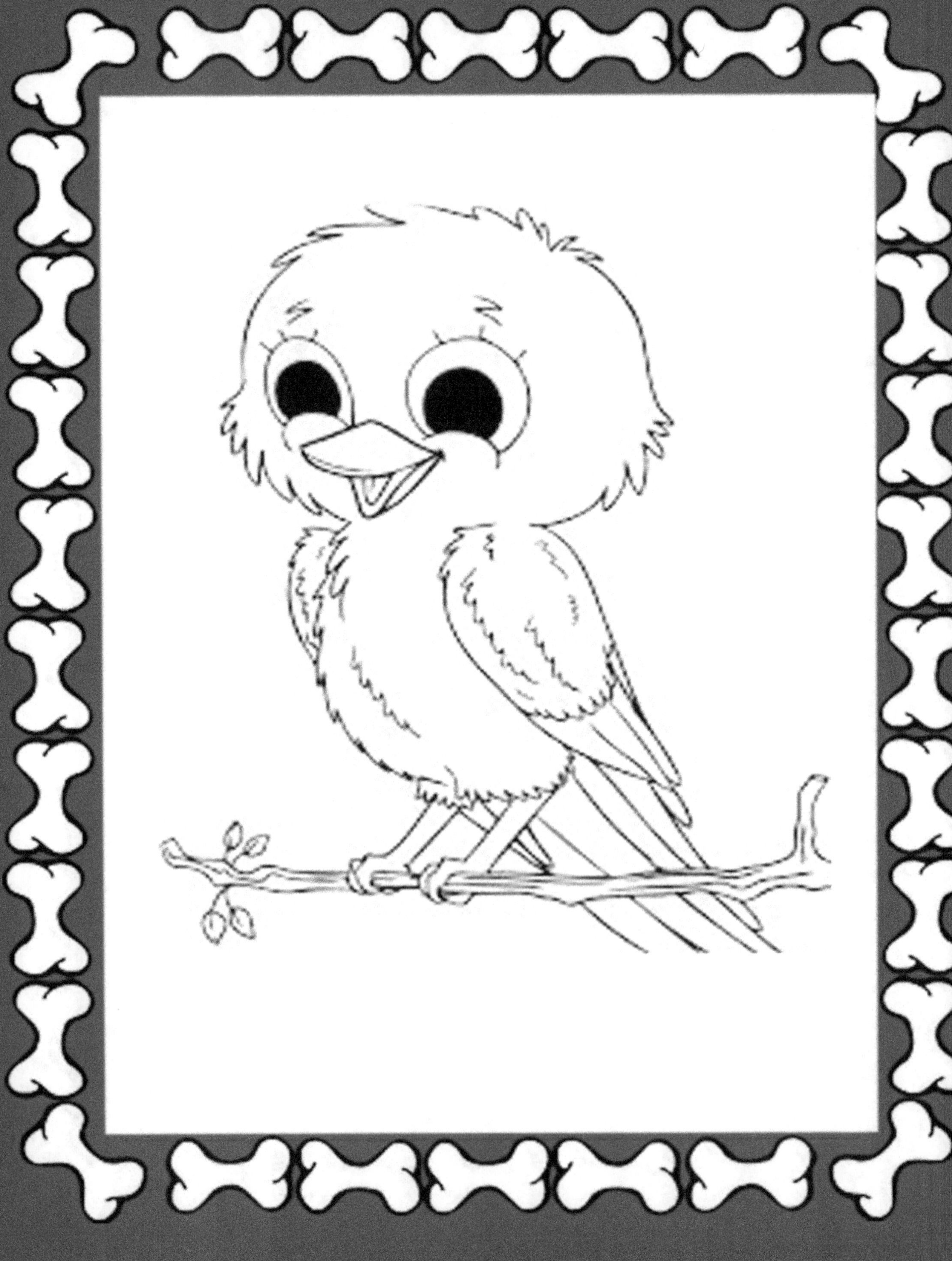

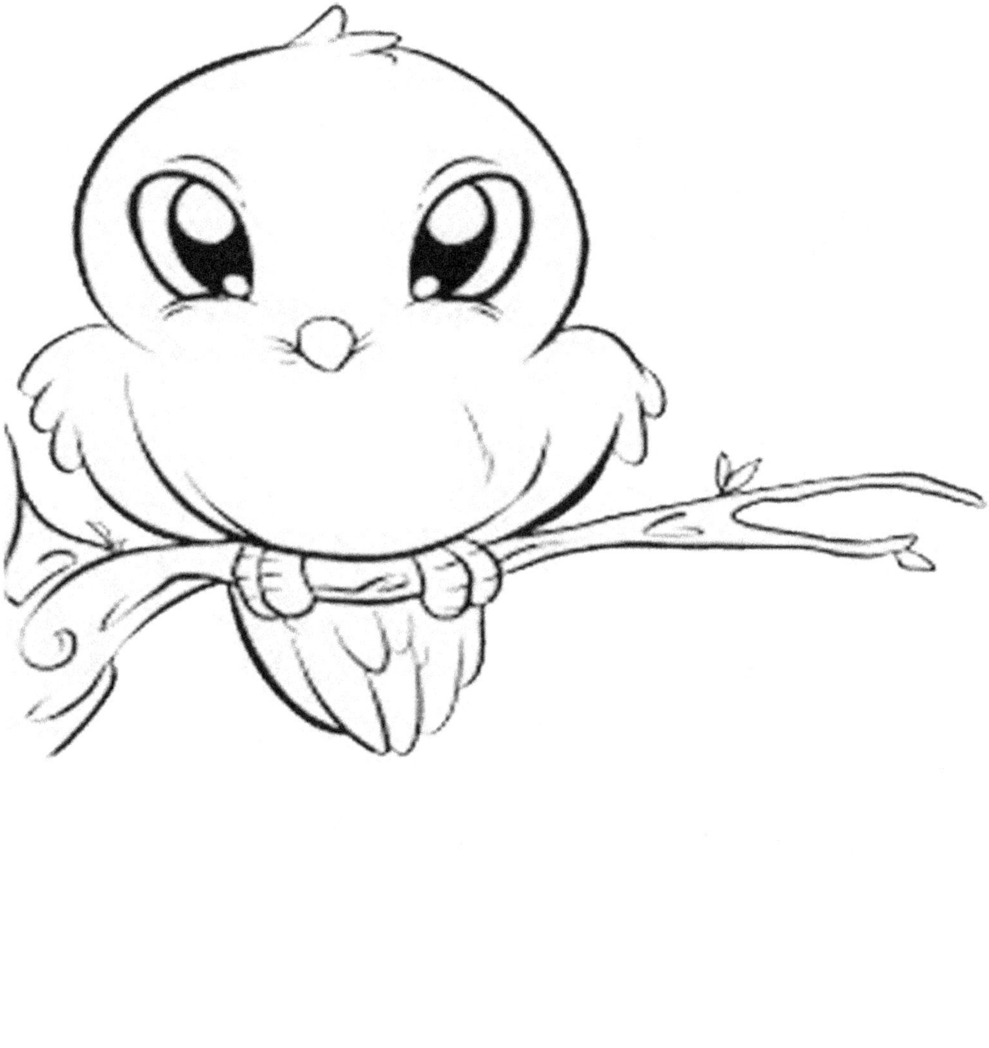

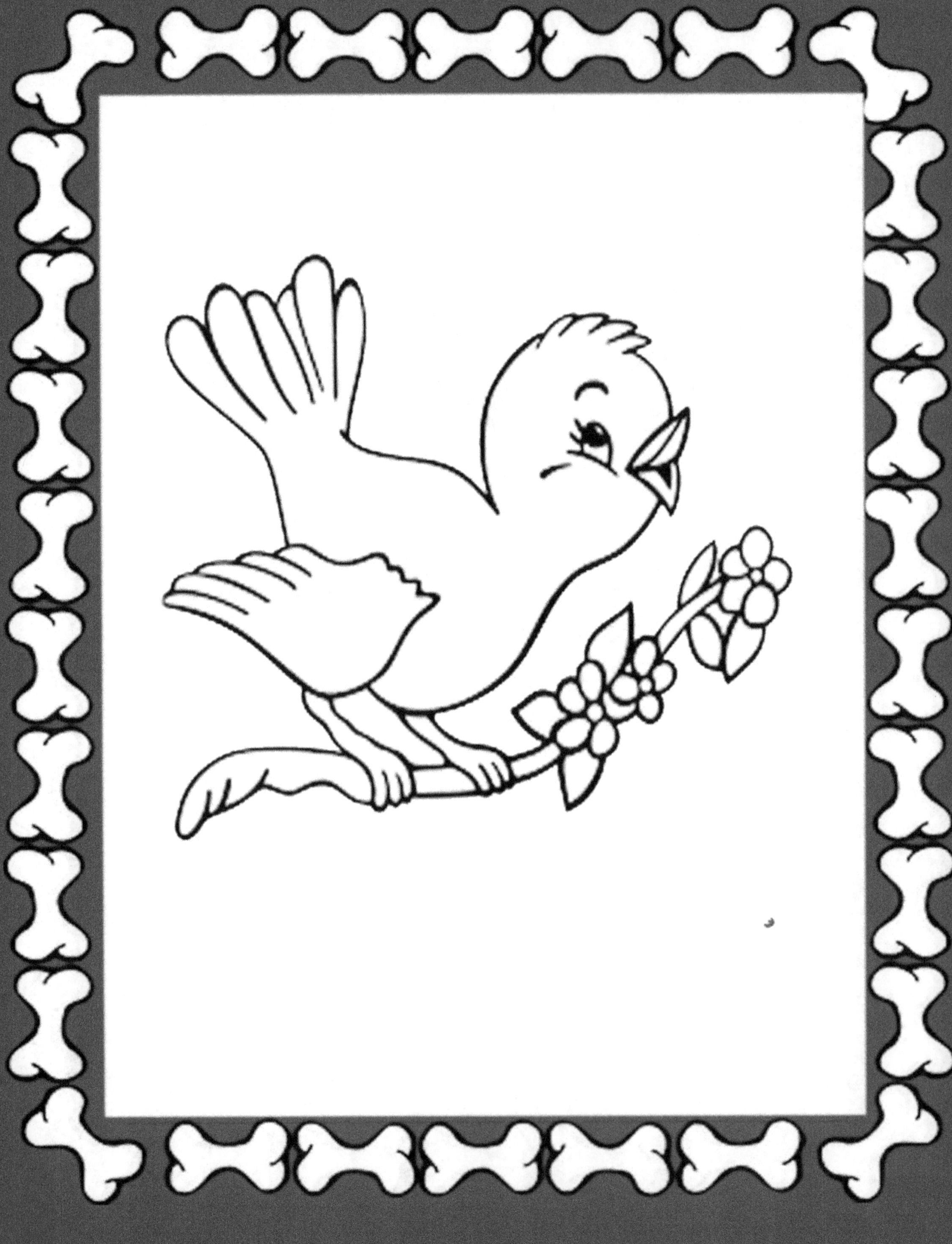

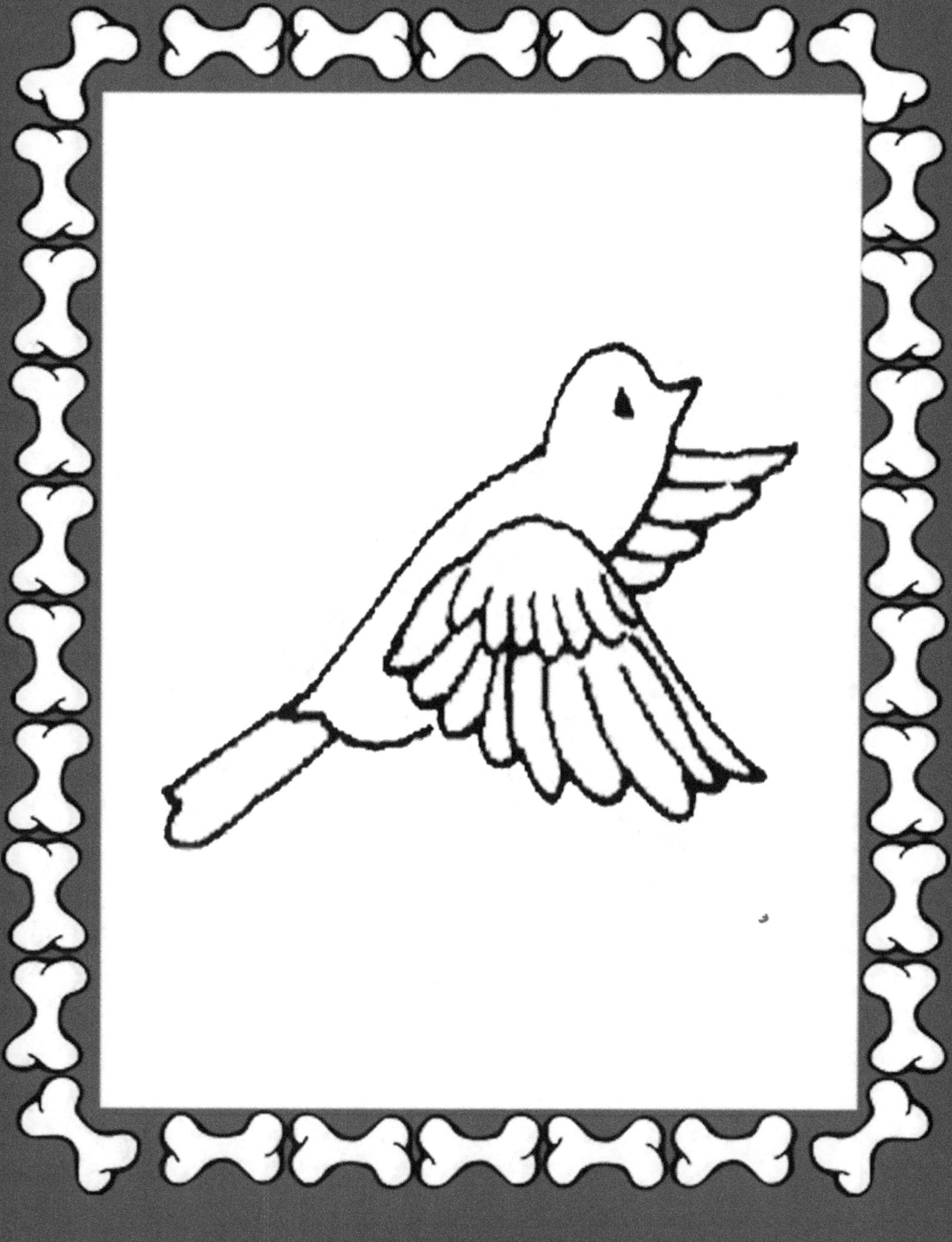

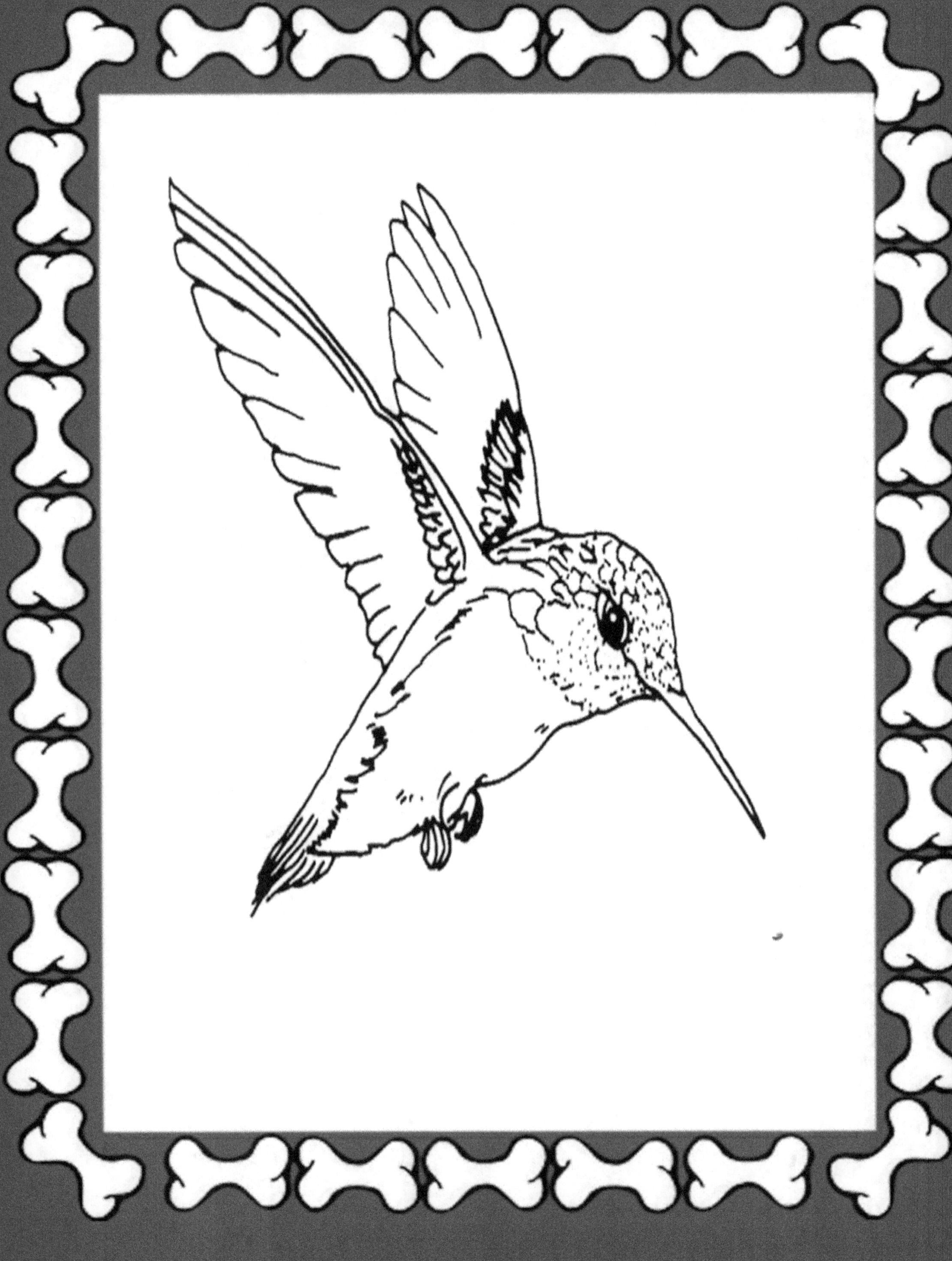

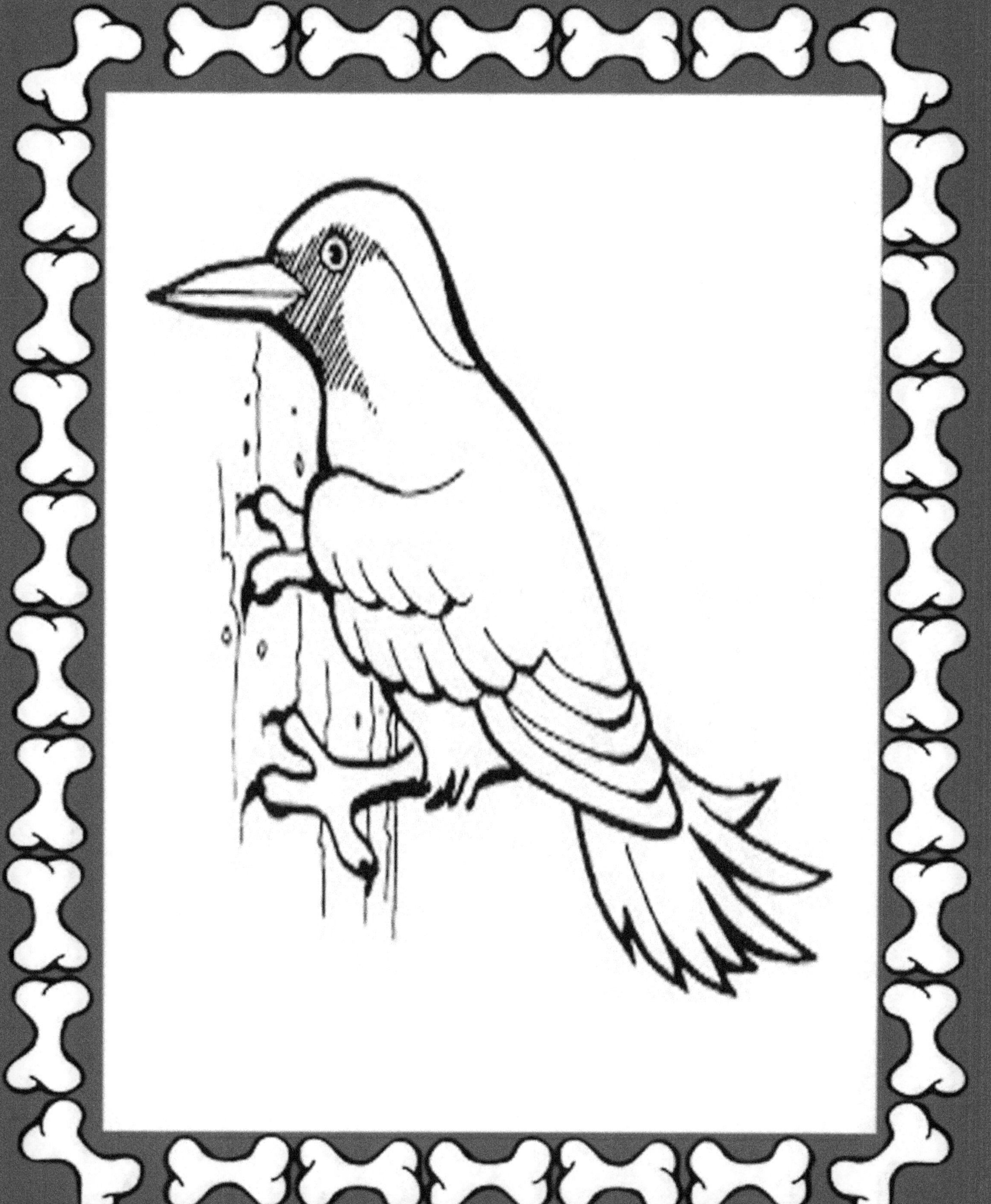

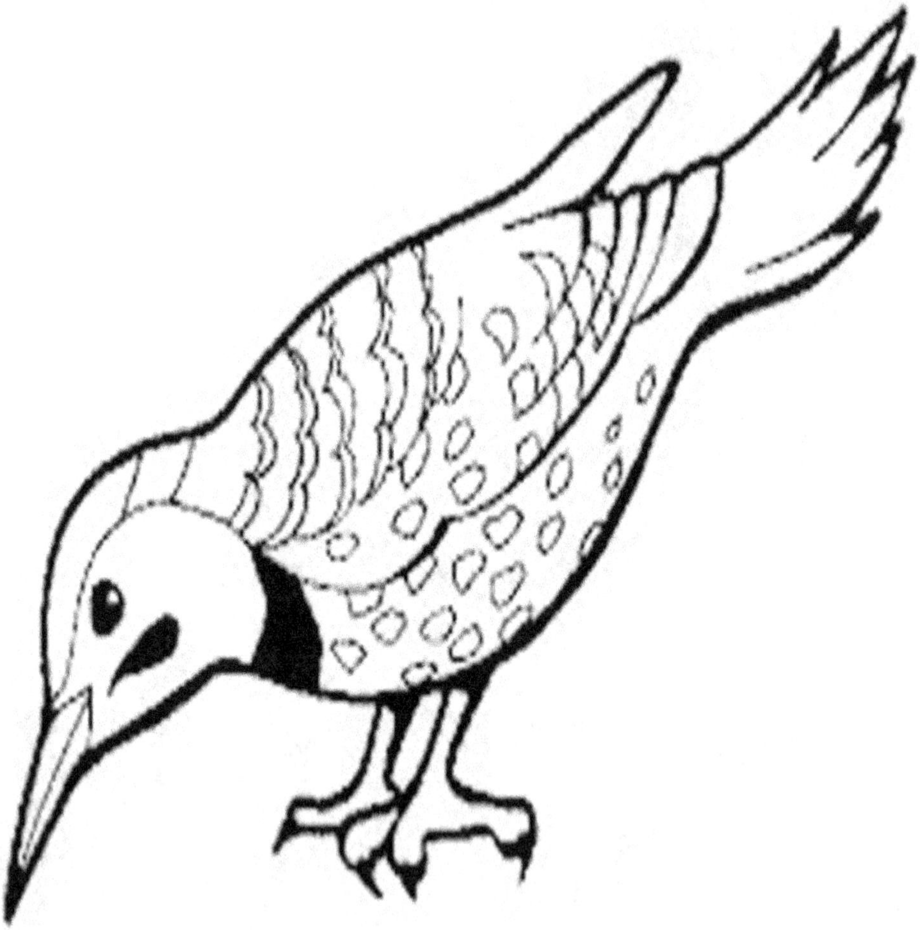

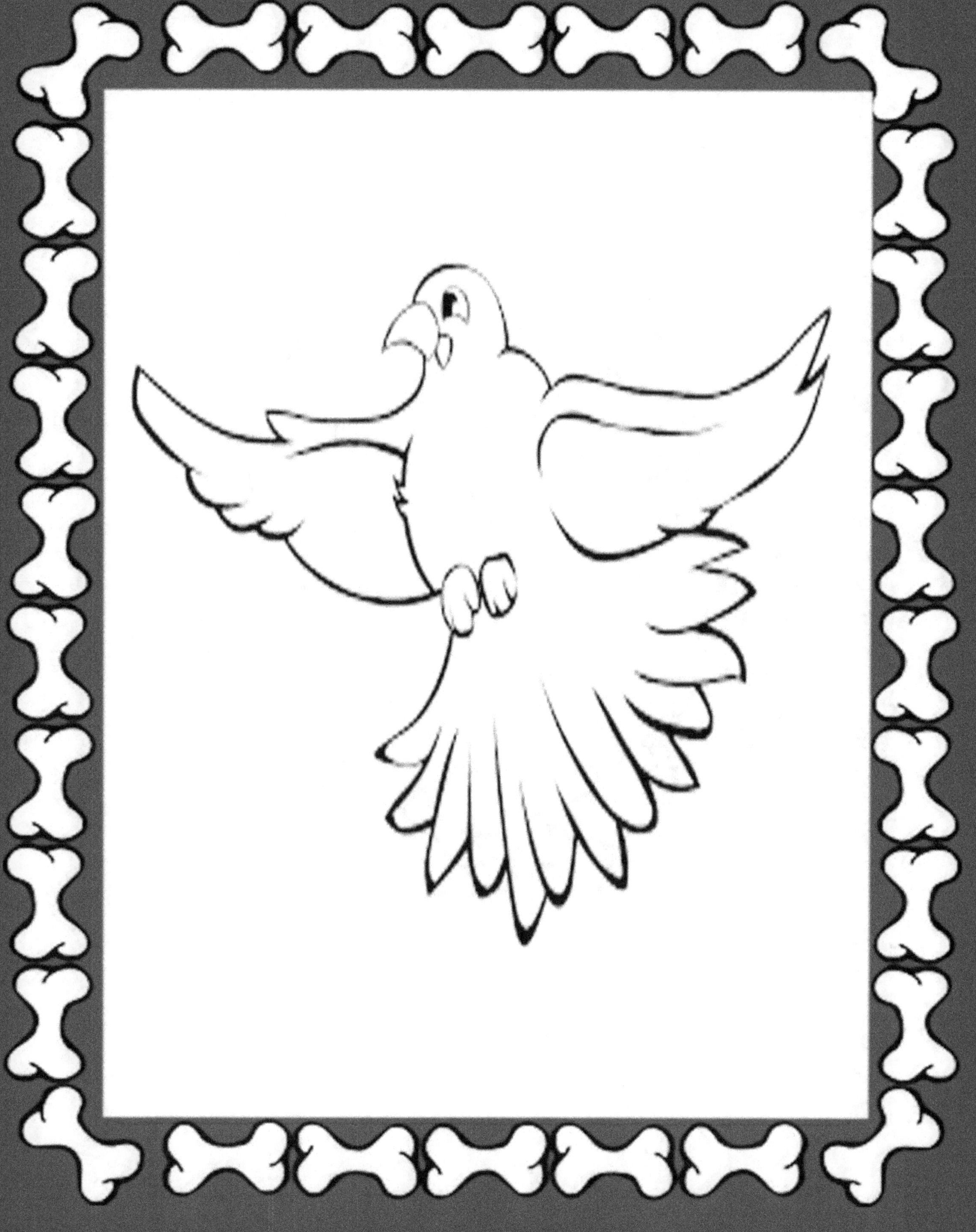

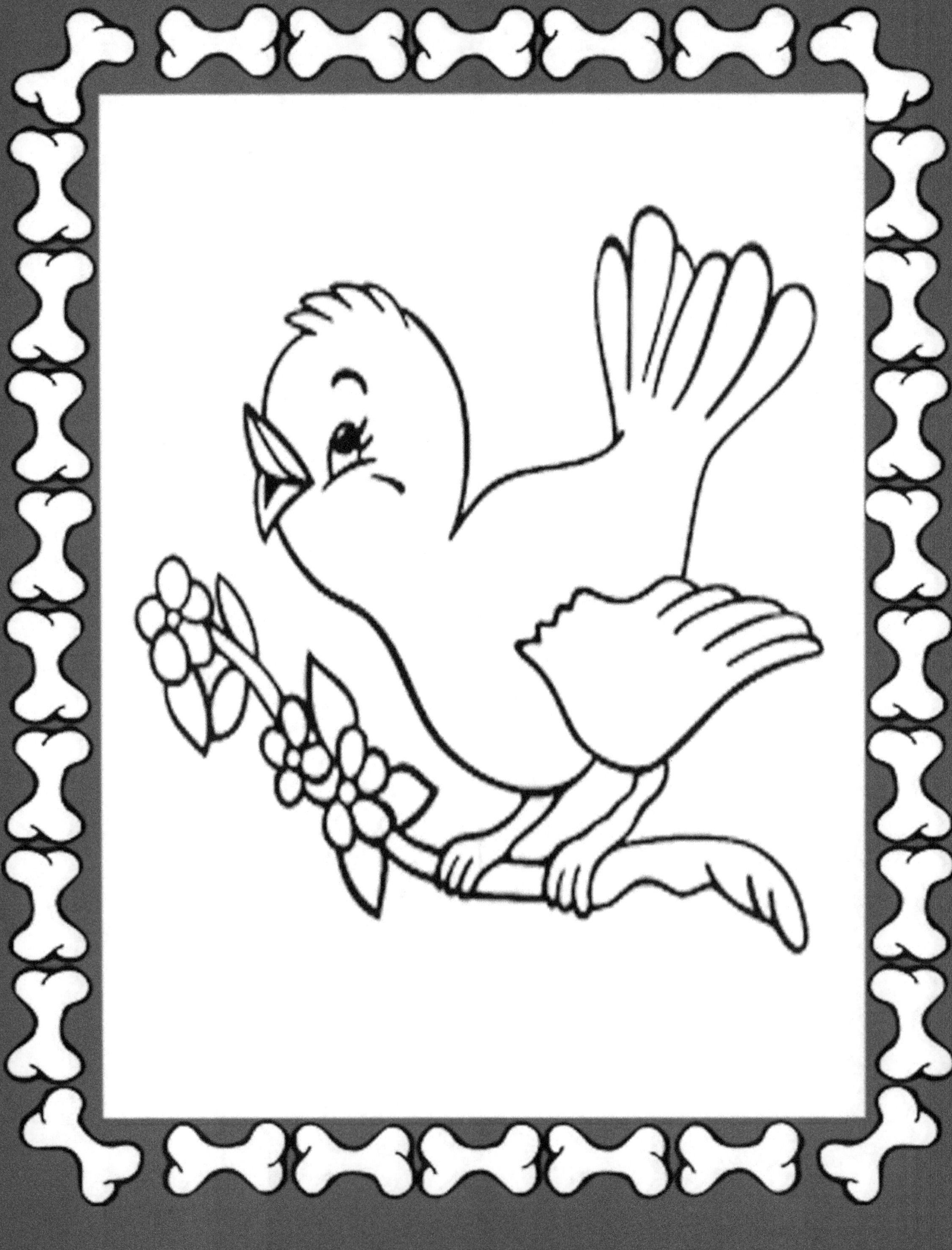

THE END

www.ingramcontent.com/pod-product-compliance
Lightning Source LLC
Chambersburg PA
CBHW080627180526
45168CB00007B/3083
* 9 7 8 1 5 0 8 6 5 9 4 3 3 *